Retro Luau

Planning the Perfect Polynesian Party

Richard Perry

COLLECTORS PRESS

PORTLAND, OREGON

Design: Wade Daughtry, Collectors Press, Inc.
Editors: Jennifer Weaver-Neist and Lisa Perry

Library of Congress Cataloging-in-Publication Data

Perry, Richard, 1960-
  Retro luau : planning the perfect Polynesian party / Richard Perry.--
1st American ed.
     p. cm. -- (Retro series)
Includes index.
  ISBN 1-888054-90-5 (hardcover : alk. paper)
 1. Cookery, Hawaiian. 2. Luaus. 3. Entertaining. I. Title. II.
Series.
TX724.5.H3P43 2004
641.59969--dc22

                          2003023406

Printed in Singapore

9 8 7 6 5 4 3 2 1

Collectors Press books are available at special discounts for bulk purchases, premiums,
and promotions. Special editions, including personalized inserts or covers, and
corporate logos, can be printed in quantity for special purposes. For further information
contact: Special Sales, Collectors Press, Inc., P.O. Box 230986 Portland, OR 97281.
Toll free: 1-800-423-1848.

Retro Luau is part of the *Retro* Series by Collectors Press, Inc.

For a free catalog write: Collectors Press, Inc., P.O. Box 230986, Portland, OR 97281.
Toll free: 1-800-423-1848 or visit our website at: collectorspress.com

Dedication

This book is dedicated to my father, Norman Perry,
for introducing me to the Hawaiian Islands and the
memorable destinations among them.

Acknowledgements

Special thanks to my wife and kids who were gra-
cious guests in my test kitchen, to my editor Jennifer
Weaver-Neist, to the staff at Collectors Press, Inc.,
to Jim Lattz for his fine illustrations, and to all my
friends who made this project possible. Warm Aloha
to you all!

Contents

Introduction

The first time Dad took the family to Hawaii was in the mid-1960s. On the flight over, I remember those miniature cologne bottles in the bathroom and the pretty stewardesses. We stayed at the Waikikian on Oahu and the Coco Palms on Kauai — the location where Elvis Presley filmed part of his movie *Blue Hawaii* just five years prior. Both hotels left me with a lasting impression of the islands, but the memories I hold dearest are the spectacular luaus we attended. They were like nothing I had seen before. Flame dancing, drumming, those little guitars, singing, girls in grass skirts, tables packed with exotic fruits, salads, desserts, and that huge pig! Everyone wore big smiles and brightly colored clothes with tropical motifs. Watching the people was half the fun!

Since those younger years, I've traveled often to the islands, renting Harley-Davidsons and body surfing from beach to beach. I usually take a few ukulele lessons (correctly pronounced "oo-koo-leh-leh" versus the mainland version "yoo-kah-lay-lee") to get me further in the island mood. There are new hotels and designer shops, and the highly evolved tourist industry offers everything from boogie boards and bicycles to scenic helicopter flights. Through all this physical evolution, the hospitality and charm of the Hawaiian people remains unchanged, and tradi-

the **Waikikian**

HAWAII'S MOST BEAUTIFUL HOTEL

tions, such as great family recipes, are still passed down through the generations. The Hawaiian Islands have a reputation as being the cultural melting pot of the Pacific. Their diverse flavors are derived from such countries as Korea, Japan, China, and The Philippines. A luau is a blend of these and other cultures and covers a wide range of food as wonderful and colorful as the people who preserve its traditions.

The luau dates back to when Polynesians first gathered for a celebration. (We're talking thousands of years ago.) The gatherings served to worship the gods, celebrate a marriage, and rejoice the birth of a child, among other things. Women, who prepared and served the food, were not allowed to attend a luau according to the Kapu system (the law). They were even forbidden to eat bananas and coconut. It wasn't until 1819, a few months after King Kamehameha I died, that the Kapu system was abolished and women were ceremoniously welcomed. We're happy they got invited! Today, women are an integral part of the luau, perhaps even overshadowing men as the iconic symbol of the ancient event: a pretty girl in a green grass skirt with a fresh flower lei around her neck.

Recreating a luau celebration in your own backyard isn't a difficult task as long as you're motivated and creative. The kids can get involved too, making their own display of kid kabobs or stringing flower leis. It should be a family event, as is the tradition: a celebration of life.

For some time, I've been gathering my favorite traditional recipes along with a few favorites from friends of the islands. What you won't find are recipes for warm air, sandy beaches, or bright sunshine. Nothing is quite like the real thing. However, with a lot of love and care, you will find that at the end of your own retro luau, you will leave your family and friends with a lasting impression of a wonderful Polynesian night.

So, throw on your favorite tropical attire — it is time for a Retro Luau!

Aloha!
Richard Perry

The author in front of the historic Waikikian Hotel on Oahu, February 1966.

Creating
That Island Atmosphere

First things first. Throw on some music by Don Ho or maybe some Hawaiian slack key guitar. Then make yourself a Mai Tai to sip on. (Hey, you've got to test the recipe yourself before the natives arrive!) Once you're in the luau mood, you're ready to roll.

Invitations

Custom invitations are fun and easy to make. One idea is to create a cruise ship or airline ticket with the luau as the destination — include location, time of arrival, and complimentary First Class service. Add a few silk flower petals and spray a whisper of floral perfume in the envelope. You can also get the kids in on the act and

use colorful paper cutouts in various shapes like palm trees and pineapples. Decorate them with stickers or colorful markers, and be sure to make a note requesting tropical attire.

Making a Lei

The lei is one of the most wonderful Hawaiian traditions. Typically made of flowers and worn like a necklace, it is a symbol of friendship and love given as a warm welcome or fond farewell. The host traditionally presents a lei to females, while the hostess does the same to males, placing the lei

around the neck and following with a kiss. Remember to add a big "Aloha!" (long "o", short "ha") as you greet your guests.

To make a flower lei, you need lots of flowers, a needle of about 2 inches, and some strong thread (#40 is nice — doubled and knotted). Some patience is helpful too!

Picking the flowers is a matter of taste, but you want flowers that mass together nicely and won't quickly wilt or bleed into clothing. The carnation and vanda orchid are among the most popular choices in the islands. Jasmine, chrysanthemums, dahlias, fuchsias, daisies, and even roses will also work.

Remove the stems just below the blossoms. If there is a green leaf bottom, loosen it to allow the flower to poof out a bit. String the flowers by pushing the needle through the top of the flower and out the base. Bunch the flowers somewhat firmly so the lei

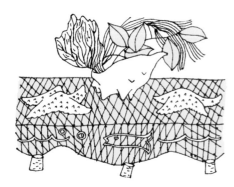

Decorations

Greenery and flowers are used to decorate the tables. Ti and banana leaves are not so easy to find on the mainland, so ferns make a nice substitute for the runner down the middle. Fishing nets, sand, blown glass floats, starfish, shells, coconuts, and small driftwood will give that nautical look, or you can keep it simple and decorate with various silk flowers. Scatter a few fresh orchids around too. Guests will sniff them all evening and can tuck a few behind their ears. (Remember that a flower behind the right ear means you're taken; a flower behind the left ear means you're romantically available.)

doesn't droop as the luau progresses, avoiding visible gaps. Upon completion, tie the ends together and dip the leis in cool water. Gently shake off the big drops and place on damp paper towels in a covered box so the air won't dry out the flowers. Store in a cool — but not ice-cold — refrigerator.

If you're allergic to flowers or have more time than money, there are fun alternatives — ones that the kids will enjoy making too. Some examples are: popcorn, weaving colorful crepe paper strips, shells, or silk flowers.

ADVENTURES IN PARADISE

featuring
ALFRED APAKA
ROY SMECK
TEROROTUA
& HIS TAHITIANS
THE ISLANDERS

Line the edges of tables with imitation hula grass to enhance the island feeling. Fire is also a big part of the luau, so use tiki torches — a safe distance from the grass skirts — to create the ambiance of a night at the

beach. Candles on the tables are a nice touch, but be careful of children. Stringing small white lights or other colorful party lights around the event is a safe alternative that adds to the festive atmosphere.

If you have some folks you want to get into the buffet line first, you can place icons, such as paper pineapples or palm trees, on each table and invite "all those with a pineapple on their table" to get the buffet line started. It is a good way to ensure that special friends and family (and perhaps the elderly) get in line before the hungry masses.

Let the island mood spill indoors as well by decorating public spaces such as your bathroom. Hang maps, tropical towels, floral photographs, and have a bowl of shell-shaped soaps. Balloons, hula girl cutouts or stickers on the mirror, and swags of artificial blooms offer additional touches to punctuate your theme.

A Record of the Event

Besides walking around with your camera, consider a staging area for photos as guests arrive. You can go all out: bring in sand and beach toys and frame the space with imitation palm trees. Or you can keep it simple and mount a retro travel poster. Just use something more interesting than the wall for the backdrop. You could always simplify and hire a photographer who can set the stage for you and sell photos afterwards. Either way, get a colorful photo album and bright-colored markers ahead of time, and ask everyone to sign the inside of the cover. Make sure you press a flower, keep an invitation, and have yourself photographed for the first page. When you add the best photos, you'll have an heirloom book for the ages!

For more information about luaus, go to our web site www.retroluau.com.

Traditional Games & More

There is more to a luau than feast and fire! Here are some activities from the Hawaiian tradition and beyond that are sure to engage guests of ALL ages and abilities. Suggested prizes include whole pineapples, fresh fruit baskets, retro posters or postcards, chocolate-covered macadamia nuts, dashboard hula dancers, and gift bags of Nut Nut Cookies or Macadamia Nut Brittle (recipes in "Sweets" section).

Coconut Bocce Ball

Paint one coconut bright red with outdoor paint and let it dry a couple of days. To start the game, give one (unpainted) coconut to each player. Toss the red coconut out into the playing field. One by one, each player tosses their coconut toward the red one, trying to get as close as possible. Whoever is closest 3 times wins the match.

Conch Blowing

Not anyone can blow a conch and make it sound like music, but many have tried! To make the conch shell a horn, cut off the apex of the shell (the spiral top). Try different lip positions to get the best sound.

Conga Line

Choose island music that boasts the best beat and start a line of dancing that snakes around the yard. Pick up dancers as you go, and keep the line connected by having each person place their hands on the person's hips in front of them. Following the leader and maintaining an unbroken line are the two greatest challenges in this activity.

The Hula

Live hula performances really complete the night. Imagine hula dancing in your own backyard! Instructors are often available for lessons, but go ahead and show off your own inventive style either way.

The graceful hula dance, in which the hands tell the story of the song, is a staple of any luau. Just turn on some Hawaiian music and follow the motions listed on the opposite page, while the feet do a couple of steps to the right, a couple to the left....

Aloha: Move hands, palms down, from the mouth to the audience.

Better take care: Waggle the right index finger while resting the right elbow on back of the left hand.

End: Bow head, extend arms forward, and cross right hand over left, palms down.

Everyone: Reach arms outward in front of chest and then spread arms apart.

Food: Make a cup with the hands and move right hand up from the cup to touch first two fingers to the lips.

Love: Cross chest with arms.

Mountain: Raise one hand over head to form the angle of a slope and the other above it to make the peak.

Rain: Raise hands above head and lower slowly while fluttering fingers.

Rainbow: Use both arms to form an arc.

Sunny day: Stretch arms to the sky while looking up.

Woman: Outline the hourglass shape of a woman using both hands.

Hula Hoop Contest

There are several ways to go about judging this contest. One involves the longest time keeping the hoop spinning around the waist. Another engages the neck, waist, arms, and legs, with winners able to spin the hoop on each body part for fifteen seconds. Master hula hoopers spin four or five hoops simultaneously while singing a Don Ho classic.

Limbo

Many associate the limbo with beach and tropics thanks to movies and television. Although it is not a traditional piece of Polynesian history, it sure is fun! All that is needed is a long pole, preferably bamboo for the tropical look. Each person bends backward at the waist, attempting to walk under the pole without touching it. Each time it gets lower until only one person can do it.

Pass the Coconut

This group game is great for kids and adults. The idea is to transfer a coconut (without dropping it) held under the chin from person to person. No hands! The last one left is the winner. Be sure to lightly sand the coconut first so it won't rub the chin.

Popcorn Lei Contest

Have one bowl of colored and one bowl of plain popcorn on a table. Each participant is given a threaded needle with the ends of the thread tied together to create a double strand. Guests judge the entries for the most beautiful lei, placing their votes on blank cards and depositing them in a closed box. The impartial hostess or host makes the final tally.

Sand Pit

Create a sand pit for the little ones by using a kiddy swimming pool or other enclosed space. Be sure to have enough tools like buckets, shovels, and molds, and provide shells and small rocks for decorating, if desired.

Treasure Hunt

The search can be as involved as you want it to be with an actual printed map or stations offering clues. Kids definitely enjoy the mystery, though adults can have fun with this too. Hide prizes around your yard or save time by placing a grand prize in the spot marked "X". This self-explained activity works well as a group sport or as an independent adventure that continues until the prizes are gone.

Tug of War

It is muscle and will versus muscle and will in the sand, on the grass, or in the dirt where you can really dig in

your feet. The court should be 16 feet long with the center of the rope marked by a colorful ribbon or tape (at the 8 foot point). Make a line in the ground at the center of the rope as well. Play as individuals or as teams, declaring a win for whichever side avoids crossing the line.

Water Balloon Toss

Preserve your tropical attire by catching — not dropping — the water balloon! Each two-person team faces each other about 8 to 10 feet apart and they toss a balloon back and forth. After each toss, each team takes a step backward and tosses the balloon again, each time getting further and further apart. Failure not only means getting wet but getting eliminated. The last dry team wins. (Don't fill the balloons until you are ready to play. Wet balloon surfaces are much more slippery.)

The Hawaiian language contains only 13 letters: A, E, H, I, K, L, M, N, O, P, U, and W. Here are some luau-related words with which you can impress your guests.

Aloha (ah-low-hah): hello or goodbye
Hale (hah-lay): home
Imu (ee-moo): the pit used for cooking the kalua pig
Kane (kah-nay): man
Kau kau (kah-oo-kah-oo): food
Lua (loo-uh): bathroom
Luau (loo-ow): the feast
Lanai (lah-nye): porch or patio
Mahalo (mah-hah-low): thank you
Nani (nah-nee): enjoyable
Ono ono (oh-noh oh-noh): delicious
Pupu (poo-poo): appetizer, finger food
Ukulele (oo-kah-leh-leh): small guitar
Wahine (vah-hee-nay): woman
Wiki wiki (vee-kee vee-kee): quickly

Getting It All Done On Time

30 Days Before: Make the master invitation list, create the menu, order chafing pans (to keep food warm), music, fresh flowers, and party decorations (especially unique items like sand, hula grass skirting, tiki lights, etc.). When ordering, mention your schedule, as you want everything to arrive a day or two (at most for the flowers) before the event. Order serving items based upon a 95% turnout. You never know who else will come unexpected, and leftover service items can always be used for other smaller events. A photographer should also be secured if you wish to go all out.

21 Days Before: Mail invitations with a 7-day advance RSVP. Don't hesitate calling those who have not responded. In today's world, people forget and reminders are often appreciated — not to mention you'll increase attendance. Order game items such as the limbo stick, conch shell, tug-o-war rope, some prizes, etc. Planning the treasure hunt and making the map early is also best done before your mind is preoccupied by food preparations. It is also a good time to figure out what you are going to wear.

7 Days Before: Finalize the guest list and get the camera ready. Follow up on ordered items that have not arrived and start preparing decorations that don't require fresh flowers. Iron and primp your outfit while making note of any missing accessories (jewelry, shoes, coconuts, etc.). Collect and store imu rocks if you are planning on cooking kalua pig. The rocks have to be absolutely dry when you heat them.

4 to 5 Days Before: Designate who will do what and when, such as decorating, cooking, serving, and cleaning. Create a shopping list and timeline for preparing the food. Start organizing games and prizes. (Remember that it takes several days for the painted coconut bocce ball to dry.)

3 Days Before: Shop for perishables and begin prep work — peeling, chopping, etc. — except for the fruit. Be sure you have plenty of ice. Get your outdoors in order, mowing and sweeping as needed. Hose off that dusty lawn furniture too!

2 Days Before: Draw a basic map where decorations, tables, and food will go. It is time for final cleaning and decoration placement inside. Digging the imu also saves time the day of the luau.

1 Day Before: Prepare remaining food, including the fruit, and store cold. Bake desserts and make leis. Use your neighbor's refrigerator if need be. And then you better invite them!

Day of the Luau: Get up early, take a deep breath, practice your hula, and begin cooking the Kalua pig and any dishes not made the day before. Start with the oven cooking first, as you may need it at the last minute. If using wood skewers, soak them in water for a few hours before grilling. Finalize decorations outside.

Most importantly, adopt the Hawaiian way by taking things nice and easy. Smile, soak in the moment, and enjoy your company. The rest will fall into place.

2

HONOLULU
BROOM
FACTORY
HONOLULU, HAWAII

The Feast

Be creative in presenting the food no matter what you decide to have on the menu. Display luau dishes in colorful bowls and platters found at specialty shops or online. Serve potato chips in a sand pail, soda pop on ice in a blow-up kiddy pool, wine and beer in an ice-filled aluminum canoe, and specialty drinks in paper tiki or coconut cups with little umbrellas and colorful straws. Have a couple bowls of fresh fruit, mixed nuts, rolls with butter, and other basics to compliment the picture and please the palate. Also keep in mind that traditional luau food was eaten with the fingers. So, if you want to be truly authentic, use only serving utensils and not eating utensils.

Serving sizes in the recipes are based upon a plate brimming with other luau foods. Some you'll find are large servings, others small. Hey, you can't please everyone! I went heavy on serving sizes for the recipes folks traditionally eat more of.

Hot spices can be added to many of the dishes, giving additional character and making them unique to you. I chose to exclude specific options since most folks like food that doesn't cause beads of sweat to build on the brow. You can always have a jug of your favorite hot sauce on hand with your own custom label that reads: ***WARNING: Luau Hot Sauce*** (or something like that).

I encourage you to be creative and play with the recipes a little. You can do minor things like exchange almonds for walnuts, double-up one fruit and remove another, or add booze to a non-alcoholic drink. The ocean's the limit. Yes, this will alter a traditional recipe, but recipes are only a guideline. You may actually come up with something you like better! So have fun, get a little crazy, and make planning this event the time of your life!

Cold Pupus

Island Fruit Kabobs

1 1/2 cups pineapple chunks
2 tbsps mint leaves, finely chopped
1 tbsp lime juice
1 large papaya
2 bananas, peeled
20 maraschino cherries
skewers

Drain pineapple, saving the juice.
Add chopped mint leaves and lime
juice to the pineapple juice. Cut
banana and papaya into 3/4-inch
chunks. Marinate fruit for 10 minutes
in pineapple juice mixture. Alternate
ingredients on skewers attractively.
Serve chilled. Makes about 20 kabobs.

Sweet Beef Chunks

1 1/2 pounds boneless beef shoulder
2 tbsps olive oil
2 tbsps brown sugar
3/4 to 1 cup water
1 tsp shallots, chopped
1 tbsp Galliano
1/2 tsp cayenne pepper
1/2 tsp salt
2 tbsps soy sauce
1/2 tsp garlic salt

Cut beef into 3/4-inch cubes, trimming off the fat. Heat oil in frying pan, add beef and sugar. Sear and sugarcoat the beef for about 5 minutes. Stir in all ingredients except garlic salt. Bring to a boil then reduce heat to medium low. Cover and cook 20 to 30 minutes, stirring often. In the last 5 minutes, remove cover and let liquid almost completely evaporate. Place beef on a baking sheet and sprinkle with garlic salt. Heat oven to 175 degrees and dry beef for approximately 45 to 60 minutes. Turn heat off and let beef cool in oven. Store covered in the refrigerator. Serves 12 to 15.

Maui Marinated Mushrooms

1/3 cup cider vinegar
1/3 cup olive oil
1/2 tsp salt
1/2 tsp white pepper
2 tsps parsley, finely chopped
1 tbsp Dijon mustard
1 tbsp brown sugar
20 to 30 fresh mushrooms

Boil all ingredients (except mushrooms)
together for 3 to 5 minutes. Add mushrooms,
reduce heat, and simmer for 5 minutes. Cool
overnight. Serves 6 to 8.

Shrimp Sushi

20 to 25 medium shrimp
1/4 cup rice vinegar
1 tbsp sugar
1/2 tsp salt

So shrimp won't curl, insert a toothpick lengthwise into each shrimp and simmer in water until just about done. Cut front open, cutting so shrimp will lie flat, and remove vein. Combine vinegar, sugar, and salt in bowl. Marinate cooked shrimp in sauce for 1/2 hour.

Sushi rice:
4 cups hot, cooked rice
1/4 cup rice vinegar
2 tbsps sugar
1/2 tbsp salt
wasabi, to taste

Combine vinegar, sugar, and salt. Bring to a boil then cool. Fold the mixture into the warm rice and let cool. Shape rice into small, football shapes slightly flattened on all sides. Put a small pinch of wasabi on top of each rice bit then add shrimp on top, pressing lightly.

Poipu Pea Salad

1 cup mayonnaise
1 cup sour cream
1/4 cup milk
2 tbsps sugar
pinch of salt
pinch of pepper
4 cups frozen peas
1 cup water chestnuts, drained and sliced
1/2 cup green onions, finely chopped

Mix together mayonnaise, sour cream, milk, sugar,
salt, and pepper. Pour mixture over peas, water
chestnuts, and green onion; let chill for 2 to 4
hours. Serves 10 to 15.

Oriental Rice Salad

1 cup long grain rice, uncooked
1 3/4 cups water
1 tsp salt
3/4 pound canned mushrooms, thinly
  sliced
1/2 cup olive oil
1/4 cup rice wine vinegar
2 tbsps soy sauce
pinch of salt
1/2 cup mandarin oranges, drained
1 cup celery, thinly sliced
2 green onions, thinly sliced
1/2 cup slivered almonds

Add rice, water, and salt together in a covered pot and bake at 350 degrees for 45 minutes. Transfer rice to a large bowl when done. Mix the oil, vinegar, soy sauce, and pinch of salt; set aside. Add mushrooms to the rice and fold in the oil mixture. Let chill for about 2 hours. At service time, gently fold in mandarin oranges, celery, green onions, and almonds. Serves 8 to 10.

Ambrosia Polynesia

3/4 cup mandarin oranges
3/4 cup pineapple chunks
3 bananas, peeled and sliced
1 cup flaked coconut
1 small jar maraschino cherries,
   rinsed and halved

Drain mandarin oranges and pineapple
chunks, saving the juice. Peel and slice the
bananas and marinate with reserved juices.
This will help avoid discoloring. Just before
serving, add coconut and maraschino cherries, mixing well with the bananas and juice.
Serves 6 to 8.

Pineapple Chicken Salad

2 cups chicken breast, cooked and
   cubed
2 cups fresh pineapple chunks
1/4 cup mayonnaise
1/4 cup sour cream
3/4 cup celery, diced
1/2 cup almonds, chopped

Combine all ingredients and let chill 2 to
3 hours before serving. Serves 10 to 12.

Macaroni Crab Salad

1 pound uncooked macaroni
3/4 pound crabmeat, chopped
1/2 cup ham, finely diced
3/4 cup frozen peas, blanched
2 stalks celery, diced
4 large hard-boiled eggs, grated
1/2 tsp sweet pickle relish
2 green onions, finely chopped
pinch of salt
pinch of pepper
2 cups mayonnaise
1 cup sour cream

Boil pasta until just barely cooked. Drain, rinse,
and cool. Add all other ingredients to the pasta.
Mix in mayonnaise and let chill for
about 8 hours. Serves 6 to 8.

Mango Fruit Salad

2 cups fresh mango, unevenly chopped
3 bananas, peeled and sliced
1 cup orange, peeled, wedged, and halved
2 oz. lime juice
3 tbsps honey
1/4 cup good quality olive oil
pinch of salt
1/4 cup fresh red cherries,
   pitted and halved

Mix and chill the fruit. Mix lime juice,
honey, and then add olive oil and salt. Toss
lightly with fruit and chill. Serves 8 to 10.

Chilled Soba Salad

1 pound soba noodles
1/2 cup carrots, grated
3/4 cup green onions, finely chopped
2 cups bean sprouts
4 cloves garlic, minced
1 tbsp ginger, minced
1/2 cup soy sauce
3 tbsps sesame oil
3 tbsps rice wine vinegar
2 tbsps honey
1 tsp chili sauce

Boil soba noodles for 1 to 2 minutes until moist
and pliable. Rinse in cool water and drain well.
Sauté carrots in sesame oil for 2 minutes, add
green onions, and cook for 1 minute more.
Transfer to a large bowl and add all ingredients
except noodles. Mix well, then add noodles and
mix well again. Chill for about 2 hours and serve.
Serves 8 to 10.

Happy Ham Salad

2 cups mayonnaise
1 cup whole milk
pinch of salt
pinch of pepper
2 cups pineapple, diced
3 cups ham, cooked and diced
1 cup red seedless grapes
1 cup green seedless grapes
1 cup celery, diced
1 cup walnuts, coarsely chopped
1 cup raisins

Combine mayonnaise, milk, salt, and pepper; set
aside. Mix all other ingredients together and
fold into mayonnaise mixture. Chill for 2 hours.
Serves 20 to 25.

Sweet Potato Salad

4 cups sweet potatoes, cooked and
  diced
3/4 pound bacon, cooked and
  coarsely chopped
2 cups pineapple chunks
3/4 cup mayonnaise
2 tbsps Dijon mustard
3 tbsps lemon juice
3/4 cup macadamia nuts, coarsely
  chopped
pinch of salt
pinch of pepper

Lightly toss sweet potatoes, bacon, and
pineapple in a large bowl. Separately
mix mayonnaise, mustard, lemon juice,
salt, and pepper. Gently fold together
all ingredients and chill for about 4
hours. Before serving, fold in
macadamia nuts. Serves 12 to 15.

Surfer's Slaw

1 head green cabbage, shredded
2 tbsps Hawaiian or Kosher salt
1 cup mayonnaise
3 tbsps cider vinegar
1 tsp fresh tarragon, finely chopped
1 cup flaked coconut
1 cup golden raisins
1/4 cup sesame seeds, toasted

Mix cabbage with salt and let rest for 2 hours. Rinse and drain thoroughly. Separately mix mayonnaise, vinegar, and tarragon. Stir in coconut, raisins, and sesame seeds. Pour mixture over cabbage and toss lightly. Chill for two hours. Serves 10 to 12.

Sunshine Salad

2 pkgs (3 oz. each) orange gelatin
1 cup hot water
1 cup orange juice
1/2 pint whipping cream
1 cup cream cheese, softened
1 1/2 cups pineapple, crushed
1 cup mandarin oranges

Mix gelatin with hot water and orange juice; let set up half way. Whip the cream and set aside. Whip gelatin and softened cream cheese together, then add whipping cream. Mix in pineapple and mandarin oranges and pour into your favorite mold. Chill and serve. Serves 8 to 10.

Hawaiian Delight

2 cups sour cream
2 tbsps sugar
2 tbsps lemon juice
2 cups pineapple chunks
2 cups celery, thinly sliced
1 cup walnuts, coarsely chopped
1 1/2 cups banana, sliced
2 cups papaya, diced

Mix the sour cream, sugar, and lemon juice
together. Gently mix in all other ingredients.
Let chill for 2 hours. Serves 15 to 20.

Pineapple Coconut Rice

3 cups long grain rice, uncooked
3 cups chicken broth
2 1/2 cups water
2 tbsps Worcestershire sauce
2 tsps salt
1 oz. butter (1/4 stick)
3/4 cup sliced almonds
2 cups sour cream
1 cup flaked coconut
2 cups canned pineapple, finely chopped
   (save the juice)
1/4 cup chives, finely chopped

Mix first 6 ingredients together in an
oven-safe pot with lid. Bake at 350 for 40
minutes. Let rest (lid on) until just warm.
Fold in sour cream, pineapple juice, sliced
almonds, flaked coconut, and chives.
Serve chilled. Serves about 20.

Pineapple Presentations

You can't have a luau without including Hawaii's signature fruit. Though pineapple is thought to have originated in Brazil, it has been a documented part of island horticulture since the 1880s. When you think Hawaii, you think pineapple, earning this symbol a distinguished place at your table.

To identify a fresh ripe pineapple, look first for a healthy crown of green leaves. A fragrant fruit is also a good indicator in addition to symmetry and excessive weight for the fruit's size. Store in a cool, humid location, and don't wait too long before eating it.

Here are some of my favorite ways to dress up a pineapple.

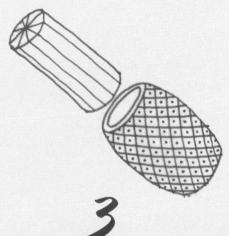

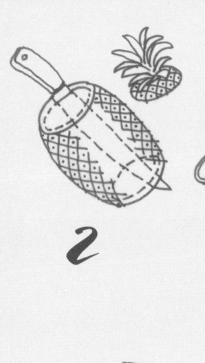

Pineapple Hideaway

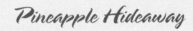

Remove bottom and crown of pineapple and save for later. Cut out fruit center in the shape of a cylinder and cut lengthwise into spears. Put spears back together to restore the cylinder and put back in the rind. Restore crown and bottom so the pineapple appears uncut. (This serves as a clever, self-service fruit dispenser displayed at various points along your buffet.)

2

3

1

4

1

2

Outrigger

Quarter pineapple lengthwise without removing the crown from each piece. Maintain the strip of core between the quarter's crown and bottom by using a curved knife to cut the fruit from the rind in one piece. Slice the removed fruit crosswise into equal sections. Replace the fruit in the rind and arrange so that every other section projects out over the edge of the rind.

3

4

Pineapple Basket

Lay pineapple on its side and remove a little less than one quarter of the fruit lengthwise. Remove a second section equal to the first, leaving an inch or so between the two. Cut out the fruit from the rind in the attached one-inch segment to form a handle. Use a curved knife to hollow out the remaining half of the fruit — with rind handle still attached — to form the bowl of the basket. Cut fruit into wedges, including the fruit from the first two segments removed, and put back into the bowl for serving.

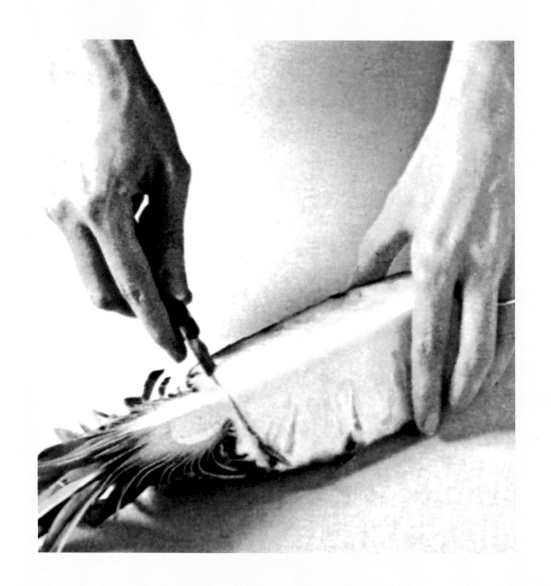

Pineapple Canoe

Cut off the bottom of the pineapple.
Quarter the pineapple lengthwise through
the crown. Cut the core from each quarter
without removing the crown. Detach the
fruit by cutting closely along the rind.
Cut 1/2-inch slices crosswise into individ-
ual pieces and display in the rind.

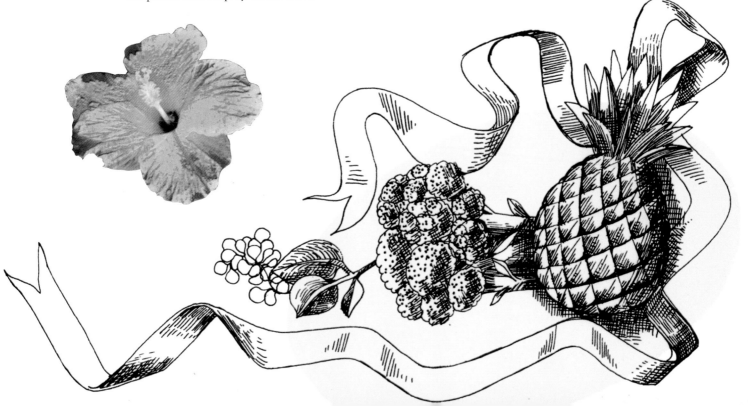

Warm Pupus

Luau Ham (with Lei)

6-pound boneless, smoked ham
1/2 cup crushed pineapple
1/2 cup pineapple chunks (or as many as
  needed for the lei)
1/2 cup brown sugar
maraschino cherries (as many as needed
  for the lei)
whole cloves

Roast the ham uncovered for 2 hours at 350 degrees. Thirty minutes before ham is done baking, score the surface 1/2 inch deep, making a crisscross pattern resembling 1-inch diamond strips, and fill with crushed pineapple. Cover strips with brown sugar and stick in whole cloves at random intersections. Return to oven for 20 to 30 minutes or until pineapple is golden brown. Stick chunks of pineapple on colored picks and arrange 1/2 inch apart in an oval pattern to resemble a lei. Between pineapple chunks, place halved cherries to complete the lei. Serves 15 to 20.

Moon Over Maui Shrimp

3 tbsps white wine
1 tbsp olive oil
3 tbsps pineapple juice
1/2 tsp onion powder
1/2 tsp garlic powder
1 tsp fresh basil, finely chopped
pinch of salt
pinch of pepper
10 slices bacon, cut in half (20 total
    pieces)
20 medium shrimp, shelled and deveined

Mix together wine, olive oil, pineapple juice, onion and garlic powders, fresh basil, salt, and pepper. Marinate shrimp overnight in sauce. Cook bacon half way, should be very pliable. Wrap bacon around each shrimp and skewer individually or grouped on a long skewer. Grill about 2 minutes each side or until bacon is evenly browned. Serves 6 to 8.

Lulu Luau Ribs

3 pounds boneless pork loin ribs
1 tbsp chopped garlic
1/2 tsp fresh ginger, chopped
1/2 cup soy sauce
3/4 cup brown sugar
1/2 cup tomato sauce
1/2 cup dark corn syrup
3 tbsps port wine
1 tbsp liquid smoke
1 tsp salt
1/4 tsp pepper

Bring all ingredients (except ribs) to a boil
then cool. Marinate ribs 4 to 6 hours. Place
ribs on rack in roasting pan filled with 1-inch
depth of water. Bake at 325 degrees for about 1
hour. Cut into about 20 1-inch pieces and
serve. Serves 8 to 10.

Keava Cabbage Rolls

10 Chinese cabbage leaves
1 tbsp cornstarch
1 cup diced chicken breast
1/4 cup bamboo shoots, diced
1 tbsp cooked green peas
2 tbsps soy sauce
1 tsp sesame oil
pinch of salt
pinch of pepper
1 tsp sesame seeds

Blanch cabbage leaves until just soft
and pliable enough for rolling. Pat
dry. Sprinkle the inside of the leaves
with cornstarch. Combine remaining
ingredients except sesame seeds and
set aside. Separate into 10 equal balls.
Place one ball on each leaf and roll
like a burrito. Steam on high heat for
15 to 20 minutes. Serve whole or
sliced, sprinkle with sesame seeds,
and offer soy sauce. Serves 8 to 10.

Killer Island Kabobs

1 pound top sirloin
1 pound boneless chicken breast
8-oz. pkg Portuguese sausage
1 can (20 1/2 oz.) pineapple chunks, drained, reserving
 juice

Marinade:
3/4 cup soy sauce
drained pineapple juice (from canned pineapple above)
2 tbsps garlic, minced
1 tbsp ginger root, minced

skewers

Cut sirloin, chicken, and sausage into roughly the same size
as pineapple chunks. Combine marinade ingredients and
marinate beef, chicken, and sausage for 2 hours. Alternate
cubes of meats with pineapple on skewers. Broil and baste
with marinade until desired doneness, about 5 minutes.
Serves 12 to 15.

Waimea Wings

2 pounds chicken wings, tips removed,
   cut at joint

Marinade:
1 tbsp salt
1 tbsp brown sugar
1 tsp fresh ginger, chopped
1 tsp fresh garlic, chopped
3 tbsps soy sauce
3 tbsps sherry

Breading:
2 cups flour
pinch of salt
pinch of pepper
4 eggs, beaten
1/4 cup water

peanut oil for frying

Combine marinade ingredients and marinate
wings 2 to 3 hours.

Season flour with salt and pepper. Separately
beat eggs and water together. Dip chicken in
flour, then in egg mixture, then back in
flour. Be sure to pat off excess flour each
time. Fry in 375-degree oil for 5 to 6 minutes, using enough oil to cover wings. Drain
well and serve warm. Serves 8 to 10.

Crab Wontons

Wonton filling:
8 oz. fresh crabmeat
1/4 cup water chestnuts, minced
3 tbsps chives, finely chopped
1 tsp port wine
1 egg, beaten
pinch of salt
pinch of pepper

1 pkg wonton papers
1 tsp cornstarch mixed with 2 tbsps water

peanut oil for frying

Mix filling ingredients until just blended. Place 1/2-teaspoon dollop into the center of each wonton wrapper. Fold as desired and seal edges using cornstarch/water mix. Fry at 375 degrees until golden brown using just enough oil to cover wontons. Serve with soy sauce. Serves 12 to 15.

Crunchy Clam Puffs

Clam topping:
3 oz. cream cheese
1 tbsp heavy cream
1/4 cup minced clams, drained
pinch of dry mustard
pinch of pepper
1/2 tsp Worcestershire sauce
1/4 tsp salt
1 tsp minced onion

24 crackers or toasted bread rounds
  (toasted 1 side)
paprika
1 tbsp chives, finely chopped

Mix clam topping ingredients. Spread on
untoasted side of the bread rounds and
broil until lightly browned. Sprinkle with
paprika and chives. Serves 10 to 15.

58

Curried Chicken Turnovers

Turnover filling:
3/4 cup chicken breast, cooked and
    finely chopped
1/3 cup cooked shrimp, minced
1 tbsp olive oil
2 tbsps water chestnuts, minced
3 tbsps mushrooms, minced
1 tbsp parsley, finely chopped

Seasonings:
1/4 tsp sugar
1/2 tsp curry powder
2 tsps soy sauce
pinch of salt

12 of your favorite flaky biscuits,
    uncooked

Heat oil and fry all ingredients (except
chicken, shrimp, and parsley) for 2
minutes. Add chicken and shrimp and
cook for 30 seconds. Turn off heat and
add parsley. Flatten biscuits to form 2
1/2-inch circles. Spoon filling evenly
among the biscuit centers and fold the
dough over to make semi-circles.
Pinch the edges to seal. Bake on an
ungreased sheet tray at 400 degrees
for 12 to 14 minutes or until lightly
browned. Serves 12 to 15.

Kalbi Kui Broiled Short Ribs

4 pounds short ribs

Marinade:
3 tbsps toasted sesame seeds
3 tbsps sesame oil
1/4 cup soy sauce
1/4 cup white onion, minced
1/3 cup green onion, finely chopped
1 tbsp garlic, minced
pinch of pepper
1 tbsp fresh ginger, minced
2 tsps brown sugar

Cut short ribs into (roughly) 2-inch pieces.
Combine marinade ingredients and marinate
ribs for 2 to 3 hours. Broil or grill for 5 to 6
minutes on each side. Serves 6 to 8.

Tempura Shrimp

24 medium shrimp

Tempura batter:
3/4 cup flour
1/4 cup cornstarch
pinch of salt
1 tbsp sugar
1 egg
1/2 cup water

peanut oil for frying

Peel shrimp leaving tails on. Cut down the back and remove vein. Place cut side down and score to prevent curling. Sift together dry ingredients. Beat eggs and water together and fold gently into dry mix. Heat peanut oil to 375 degrees. Dip shrimp by the tail into the batter making sure to coat entire shrimp evenly. Place in the hot oil and cook for 4 to 5 minutes. Shrimp should be medium to golden brown when done. Serves 6 to 8.

Ricky's Lemon Chicken

1 pound chicken breast meat, cut into 1-inch cubes

Marinade:
1/2 tsp salt
2 tbsps white wine
2 tbsps soy sauce
1 tsp lemon juice
1 tsp sugar

Batter:
2 eggs
1/4 cup flour
1/4 cup cornstarch
1/2 tsp baking powder

olive oil for frying

Lemon sauce:
1 tbsp olive oil
1 tsp salt
1/3 cup sugar
2 tbsps cornstarch
1/4 cup lemon juice
1 1/2 cups chicken broth
1/2 tsp garlic powder
lemon slices for garnish

Combine marinade ingredients and marinate chicken for 30 minutes. Beat eggs, flour, cornstarch, and baking powder into a smooth batter. Heat oil to 375 degrees. Coat chicken pieces with batter and deep fry for about 5 minutes until golden brown. Drain on paper towels.

To make lemon sauce:
Heat oil and add remaining sauce ingredients. Stir constantly until sauce is thick and translucent. Pour sauce over chicken and garnish with lemon slices. Serves 10 to 12.

Aloha Chicken

1 pound dark chicken meat

Marinade:
1/2 tsp salt
2 tbsps white wine
2 tbsps soy sauce
1 tsp lemon juice
1 tsp sugar

Batter:
2 eggs
1/4 cup flour
1/4 cup cornstarch
1/2 tsp baking powder

olive oil for frying

Pineapple sauce:
1 tbsp olive oil
1 tsp salt
1/4 cup sugar
2 tbsps cornstarch
1/2 cup pineapple juice
1 1/2 cups chicken broth

maraschino cherries, halved, for
    garnish
1/2 cup fresh pineapple, crushed

Combine marinade ingredients and marinate chicken for 30 minutes. Beat eggs, flour, cornstarch, and baking powder into a smooth batter. Heat oil to 375 degrees. Coat chicken pieces with batter and deep fry for about 5 minutes until golden brown. Drain on paper towels.

To make pineapple sauce:
Heat oil and add remaining sauce ingredients. Stir constantly until sauce is thick and translucent. Pour sauce over chicken and garnish with maraschino cherries and crushed pineapple. Makes about 12 servings.

Macadamia Cheese Puffs

4 oz. cream cheese
3 tbsps mayonnaise
2 tbsps chives, finely chopped
3 tbsps macadamia nuts, chopped
1/4 tsp salt

Soften cream cheese and mix with remaining
ingredients. Spread on crackers or small
toasted bread slices and broil 1 minute or
until delicately brown. Serves 8 to 10.

Polynesian Beef Jerky

1 2-pound flank steak

Marinade:
1/4 cup soy sauce
2 tbsps brown sugar
1 tsp garlic, minced
1 tsp ginger root, minced

Pound steak on thick end to even
thickness. Cut into 2 x 4-inch strips.
Combine marinade ingredients and
marinate beef strips for 4 hours.
Place on a rack in a shallow roasting
pan and bake at 225 degrees for 6
hours. Slice thin and serve.
Serves 8 to 10.

Ribs in Pineapple-Mustard Sauce

4 pounds pork spareribs
1/2 tsp salt
1/2 tsp pepper
1 tsp garlic powder
3 tbsps butter
1 onion, finely chopped
1/3 cup brown sugar
1/4 cup Chardonnay wine
1/3 cup Dijon mustard
2 cups pineapple, chopped small
2 tbsps parsley, chopped

Place ribs on rack in baking pan. Season with salt, pepper, and garlic powder. Bake at 350 degrees for 45 minutes to 1 hour. Melt butter in a skillet and sauté onion until transparent. Add sugar, wine, and mustard. Bring to a low boil, reduce heat, and stir in pineapple. Pour over ribs. Bake at 375 degrees for about 15 more minutes. Serves 10 to 12.

Shrimpy Toast

1 pound small bay shrimp, minced

1/3 cup onion, minced

1/3 cup water chestnuts, minced

1 tbsp chives, finely chopped

1 egg, beaten

1/2 tsp salt

1 tsp sugar

1 tbsp cornstarch

1 tsp port wine

1/2 tsp sesame seed oil

10 slices white or sourdough bread

peanut oil for frying

Mix all ingredients together except bread and peanut oil. Trim crust from bread. Spread with shrimp mixture evenly among the 10 slices. Cut each slice into 6 pieces. Heat oil to 375 degrees and fry pieces shrimp side down until edges are toasted. Turn over and fry until golden brown. Drain and serve hot. Serves 15 to 20.

Classic Stuffed Mushrooms

50 fresh mushrooms, stems removed (save)

1 tbsp chives, minced

1 tbsp butter

1/2 tsp salt

pinch of white pepper

8 oz. cream cheese, softened

Wash and dry mushrooms. Mince mushroom stems and sauté with chives in butter. Add salt and pepper then set aside to cool. Add mixture to cream cheese and beat fluffy. Fill mushroom caps and place on lightly-greased baking sheet. Bake at 375 degrees for 10 to 12 minutes until tops are lightly brown. Serves 10 to 12.

Beachside Barbecue Shrimp

Marinade:

1/3 cup tomato sauce

1/4 cup soy sauce

3 tbsps brown sugar

1/4 tsp crushed red pepper

1 tbsp ginger root, minced

1 tbsp garlic, minced

1/4 cup chives, minced

2 pounds medium shrimp, shelled and deveined

skewers

Combine marinade ingredients. Skewer shrimp and marinate for 4 hours. Broil about 5 minutes or until done. Serves 15 to 20.

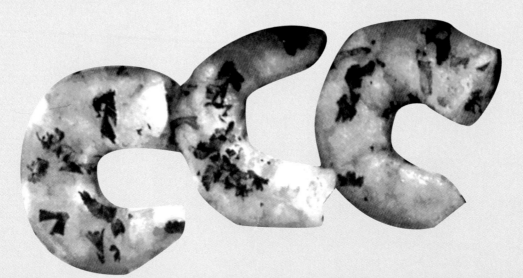

Perfect Pork Dumplings

Filling:
2/3 pound ground pork
1/4 cup minced green onion
1 egg, beaten
2 tsps brown sugar
1/2 tsp salt
pinch of pepper

24 wonton wrappers

Combine all filling ingredients and mix well. Place 1 tablespoon filling into center of each wonton wrapper. Moisten edges of wrappers and gather around filling. Pinch lightly to enclose the filling while leaving the top open. Steam on wax-paper-lined steamer for 15 to 20 minutes and serve with soy sauce. Serves 8 to 10.

Sweet & Sour Meatballs

2 pounds ground beef

2 eggs

1/4 cup cornstarch, divided

1/3 cup onion, minced

1/2 tsp nutmeg

1 tsp salt

pinch of pepper

1 tsp garlic powder

3 tbsps olive oil

1 1/2 cups pineapple juice

2 tbsps soy sauce

1/4 cup rice wine vinegar

1/2 cup brown sugar

2 cups pineapple chunks

2 green bell peppers, cut into 1-inch pieces

Mix together beef, eggs, 1 teaspoon corn starch, onion, nutmeg, salt, pepper, and garlic powder. Form mixture into 1-inch balls. Heat oil in a skillet and brown meatballs on all sides. In a large saucepan, add remaining cornstarch to pineapple juice, soy sauce, vinegar, and brown sugar. Bring to a boil, stirring constantly. If too thick, add small amount of water. Add meatballs, pineapple, and green bell pepper and simmer 5 minutes. Serves 12 to 15.

Lava Pork Tenderloin

2 pounds whole pork tenderloin
   (or 2 1-pound pieces)
1/4 cup brown sugar
2 tsps salt
1/3 cup honey
2 tsps soy sauce
2 tbsps Riesling wine
1 tbsp red food coloring
1/2 cup water

Rub tenderloin with brown sugar. Combine remaining ingredients and marinate pork for at least 12 hours in refrigerator. Drain pork and place on a rack over about 1 inch of water. Bake at 350 degrees 1 1/2 hours. Turn every 15 minutes and baste with remaining sauce. Slice thin and serve warm or cold. Serves 10 to 12.

Sweet Sour Pork

2 pounds boneless pork chop, cut in 1-inch
  cubes
2 tsps salt
2 tsps sherry
1 tbsp soy sauce
1/3 cup cornstarch
1/4 cup olive oil

Sauce:
3/4 cup brown sugar
1 cup cider vinegar
3 tbsps tomato sauce
3/4 cup pineapple juice
1 tbsp soy sauce
2 tbsps cornstarch

Combine pork, salt, sherry, soy sauce, and
cornstarch and set aside for 20 minutes.
Heat oil and brown pork until golden
brown on all sides, cooking 1/2 way (about
5 minutes). Mix sauce ingredients together
and add to pork. Simmer 5 minutes and
serve. Garnish with optional pineapple
chunks. Serves 15 to 20.

Asian Chicken Kabobs

1 pound chicken breast, boned and
   cut into 3/4-inch pieces
1 can water chestnuts, drained
1 bell pepper, seeded and cut
   into 3/4-inch pieces

Marinade:
1/4 cup soy sauce
1/4 cup brown sugar
1/4 cup sake

skewers

Alternate chicken, water chestnuts, and bell pepper on
skewers. Combine marinade ingredients and marinate
kabobs 30 minutes. Broil for about 6 to 8 minutes,
turning once and basting often with marinade.
Serve hot. Serves 12 to 15.

Teriyaki Beef Skewers

2 pounds top sirloin

Marinade:
1 cup brown sugar
1 cup soy sauce
1/2 cup sake
2 tbsps garlic, minced
1 tsp ginger root, minced

skewers

Cut sirloin into thin strips about 4 inches long.
Mix marinade ingredients together and marinate
for 1 hour. Thread sirloin strips onto skewers by
weaving in and out. Broil or barbecue for about
4 minutes, turning once and basting occasionally.
Serve hot. Serves 15 to 20.

Drunken Coconut Shrimp

1 cup flour
2 pounds medium shrimp, shelled and
  butterflied (split down the back)
1/2 cup amber or dark beer
2 eggs
1 cup coconut flakes
1 quart peanut oil

Place flour in a small bowl. Beat eggs and mix in beer. Coat shrimp in flour, pat
off excess, then dip into egg/beer mixture. Immediately roll in coconut flakes
and deep fry in 350-degree peanut oil for about 2 minutes or until coconut is
golden. Do not let coconut get too brown. Serves 8 to 10.

Serve with the following sauce.

Pineapple dipping sauce:
6 oz. pineapple juice
1 tbsp sugar
2 tbsps honey
2 tsps corn starch
pinch of dried red chilies
2 tsps lemon juice

Mix all ingredients well and heat until boiling, stirring constantly. Turn off heat,
let cool to room temperature, then chill until serving time.

Cooking a Kalua Pig

While other cooking methods are good — really good — imu pig is out of this world. The texture and flavor of a pig cooked underground can only be described by actually experiencing it. If authenticity is what you're about, this method is sure to please. Just make sure you allow a good 12 to 13 hours of time for the process, as it is a slow and careful one.

Although preparing and cooking the pig is fairly simple, attention to detail is important. Assuming you have located ti or banana leaves, you will also want to contact your local fire department and make sure you can build a small pit fire in your backyard. They like to know about these things!

Dig a 2-foot deep, oval-shaped pit large enough to accommodate the pig comfortably. Fill it with smooth igneous rocks (rocks that are formed from a molten state like lava). IMPORTANT: These rocks need to be dense and completely dry or they could pop when heated and cause serious damage! For extra safety, store the rocks in a dry location and consider digging the fire pit a day or two in advance. This eases the pressure of final tasks the day of the luau.

Build a fire of hardwood in the pit, gradually building up to large pieces of wood. Koa and kiawe wood are used in Hawaii, though cherry and mesquite offer mainland alternatives.

Lay rocks on the fire — enough to cover the entire base of the pit — and monitor as the fire begins to heat the rocks. While you wait, mash banana stalks with a sledgehammer and keep moist along with banana or ti leaves. Move the cleaned pig to a sanitized, flat surface near the fire and place on chicken wire cut large enough to encase the entire pig.

When the fire has turned to coals and the rocks have turned white, remove any larger pieces of wood and create a level bed with what remains. Use tongs to place three or four large, hot rocks (brushed free of ash) inside the open cavity of the pig. Wrap loosely with chicken wire to ensure easy

transportation, even cooking, and stability when removing from the imu. Next, place mashed banana stalks on the exposed rocks or use the moistened banana leaves (not dripping wet) if you cannot locate the stalks. Place the pig on the bed and cover with banana leaves, completely encasing it. (This is steaming hot work!) Then cover the pig with damp canvas tarps and pile on the dirt. The mound should be about 3 feet high with no steam leakage. Sand works great as the final covering.

Cook the pig for about 10 hours — basically all day but not less than 8 hours for a 100-pound pig. This feeds about 150 people, considering all the other goodies, but smaller pigs are available for smaller luaus. A 50-pound pig will serve 60 to 75 people. Upon removal from the pit, be sure to get all of the dirt off the tarps before pulling out the pig. Carefully remove

the tarps and then the leaves. (Be careful, they're hot!) Carry the pig by the wire mesh back to the staging area where your chafing pans await. Open the mesh and remove the rocks. You are now ready to serve a Polynesian tradition!

If you are unable to devote the extra time and energy required with imu cooking, there are several alternatives that still make for a memorable feast.

Wiki Wiki (Quick) Oven Method

4 pounds pork butt (shoulder)
2 cups water
2 tsps liquid smoke (more or less for varied smokiness)
2 tbsps Hawaiian or Kosher salt

Score the pork all over with a knife. Rub meat thoroughly with salt and liquid smoke. Pour water into roasting pan or other deep pan with a lid. Place the pork into the pan, fat side up, as it provides additional moisture and flavor to the meat. Bake in a 375-degree oven with the lid on for 3 hours. If you have more time, you can slow roast the pork at 325 degrees for 3 1/2 to 4 hours or at 300 degrees for 4 to 5 hours, checking it for tenderness after 3 hours. The longer time is recommended since it is never good to rush the process. When done, meat should easily pull away with a fork. Remove the fat on top and shred pork with a fork. If you overcook the meat (Hey, we all make mistakes!) or it's gotten a bit too dry from early preparation, add a few splashes of hot water mixed with a couple tablespoons of olive oil. Serves 6 to 8.

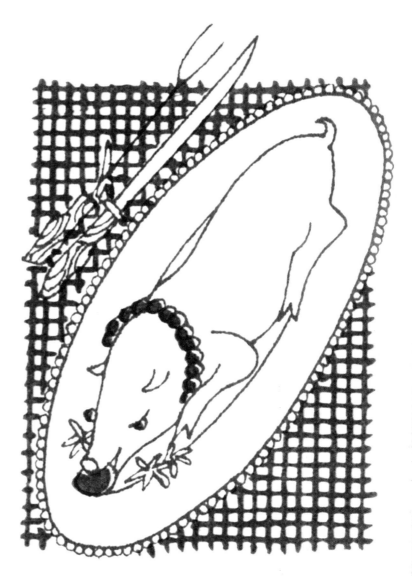

Slow Smoker Method

If you have a smoker, this is a great method to get that kalua pig flavor without digging a pit. The juices (and, yes, the fats) get trapped inside the ti or banana leaves that are wrapped around the pork. The slow-cook method is similar to the benefits of slow roasting a large prime rib: tender and juicy.

The first thing you need to do is call around and make sure you can get ti or banana leaves. I called a local Asian market and they had both in stock. The leaves can also be purchased online.

Using the same measurements as in the Wiki Wiki Oven Method, rub meat thoroughly with salt and liquid smoke. Wrap with leaves (first removing the center ribs) and secure with twine. It's best to let the meat sit for a few hours to absorb the seasoning before smoking. Place the pork inside a shallow roasting pan with a cup or two of water, and smoke at 225 degrees for 6 hours. Remove the leaves. The meat should shred easily with a fork. Serves 6 to 8.

Chips, Dips, & Spreads

Potato Chips

4 medium potatoes, peeled
1 quart peanut oil
pinch of salt

Cut potatoes paper-thin. Store in cold,
salted water for 6 to 8 hours. Heat oil to
375 degrees and fry until golden brown.
Drain onto paper towels and season with
salt while still warm. Serves 12 to 15.

Coconut Chips

1 coconut, skinned, meat removed
1 quart peanut oil
pinch of salt

Using a peeler, slice coconut paper-thin. Spread out on an ungreased sheet tray. Bake at 350 degrees for 30 to 40 minutes or until crisp and lightly brown. Sprinkle with salt and serve. Serves 12 to 15.

Green Nanner Chips

6 green bananas
1 quart peanut oil
pinch of salt to taste

Peel bananas and thinly slice diagonally. Fry at 375 degrees until golden brown. Drain onto paper towels and season with salt while warm. Serves about 12 to 15.

Cold Shrimp Dip

16 oz. cream cheese, softened and
  whipped
2 cups bay shrimp
1/2 cup mayonnaise
1 cup chili sauce
1/3 cup onion, finely chopped
1 tsp Worcestershire sauce
few drops of Tabasco or hot sauce
crackers or toasted bread

Gently fold all ingredients together
until well blended. Refrigerate at least
4 hours. Serve with crackers or toasted bread. (NOTE: Freezes well.)
Serves 10 to 12.

Avocado Crab Dip

3 large, ripe avocados, diced
2 tbsps fresh lemon juice
1/3 cup onion, finely diced
2 tbsps Worcestershire sauce
10 oz. cream cheese, softened
1 cup sour cream
1 tsp salt
1 pound fresh crabmeat

Lightly toss avocado with lemon juice,
onion, and Worcestershire. Mix in softened cream cheese, sour cream, and salt.
Carefully fold in crabmeat. Chill and
serve with crackers or toasted bread.
Serves 12 to 15.

Sun-Dried Tomato Cream Cheese

16 oz. cream cheese, softened
1/4 cup hydrated sun-dried tomatoes, finely
   chopped
1/2 cup mayonnaise
1/2 tsp garlic powder

Combine and mix ingredients thoroughly.
Serves 6 to 8.

Mango Chutney

6 mangos, peeled and diced
1 red bell pepper, finely diced
1/2 cup onion, finely diced
2 apples, peeled and diced
1/2 cup raisins
1/2 cup sugar
1 1/4 cups white wine vinegar
1/2 tsp mustard powder
1 tsp coriander seed
1/4 tsp red chili peppers
1 tsp salt
1 tsp pepper

Mix all ingredients and store chilled for 8 hours. Heat in saucepan at slight simmer for 45 minutes. Chill for 3 to 4 hours. Serves 10 to 12.

Cream Cheese With Mango Chutney

16 oz. cream cheese, softened and whipped
2 cups mango chutney (see recipe)

Gently fold all ingredients together until well blended. Refrigerate at least 4 hours. Serve with crackers or toasted bread. (NOTE: Freezes well.) Serves 8 to 10.

Macadamia Crab Dip

16 oz. cream cheese, softened
16 oz. crabmeat, divided
2 tbsps milk
1/2 tsp Worcestershire sauce
1/2 cup green onion, finely chopped
2 tbsps chopped macadamia nuts

Combine all ingredients, reserving
half the crabmeat, and beat until light
and fluffy. Gently fold in the remaining crab. Spread evenly in a shallow
baking pan and bake at 400 degrees
until top is lightly browned and bub-
bly, about 6 to 8 minutes. Serve with
crackers, chips, or toasted bread.
Serves 10 to 12.

Hors d'Oeuvre Combinations With Cream Cheese

Mix 16 ounces whipped cream cheese with any of the following to create a tasty spread. Serve with pumpernickel or rye bread, toasted rounds, or assorted crackers. Serves 6 to 8.

* Chopped smoked oysters and macadamia nuts
* Diced avocado pulp and curry powder
* Anchovy paste and Worcestershire sauce
* Grated cucumber, chopped chives, and sour cream
* Mashed sardines in oil and chopped chives
* Horseradish and minced onion

Island Cheddar Spread

16 oz. cream cheese, softened
4 cups medium cheddar cheese, shredded
1/2 cup port wine
1 tbsp seasoning salt
1 tsp garlic powder
1 tsp hot dry mustard
24 oz. crushed pineapple, drained
1/4 cup parsley, minced

Whip softened cream cheese with cheddar and port wine until smooth and light. Add seasoning salt, garlic powder, and mustard. Fold in pineapple and parsley. Chill for 1 hour. Serves 10 to 12.

Smoked Salmon Spread

16 oz. cream cheese, softened
8 oz. smoked salmon, flaked
3 tbsps lemon juice
1/4 cup chives, finely chopped
pinch of salt
pinch of pepper
1/2 tsp garlic powder
1 cup tomato, diced

Mix whipped cream cheese with salmon, lemon juice, chives, salt, pepper, and garlic powder. Fold tomato in gently and chill overnight for best flavor. Good spread for crackers. Serves 8 to 10.

Curried Spread

1 cup pineapple, chopped small
1/2 cup sour cream
1/2 cup mayonnaise
1/4 cup heavy cream
1 tsp curry powder
1 tsp garlic powder

Combine all ingredients and mix well. Chill overnight before serving. Serve with crackers or toasted bread. Serves 6 to 8.

Pineapple Mango Pate

16 oz. cream cheese, softened and
  whipped
2 large mangos, peeled and pitted
2 cups crushed pineapple, drained
16 oz. jar pineapple chutney

Mix softened cream cheese with fresh
mango in blender. Spread evenly onto a
shallow serving platter or tray. Mix
pineapple and chutney. Spread mixture
evenly over cream cheese. Serve with
crackers or toast. Serves 12 to 15.

Beer Cheese Spread

1 pound medium cheddar cheese
1 pound jack cheese
1 tbsp garlic powder
1 tbsp Worcestershire sauce
1/4 tsp dry mustard
1/2 tsp salt
1/2 tsp hot pepper sauce, optional
10 oz. beer

Blend cheeses with all ingredients, slowly adding the beer. Chill for 4 hours. Serve with chips and crackers. Serves 10 to 12.

Spicy Avocado Dip

2 ripe avocados
2 tsps lemon juice
1/2 tsp Worcestershire sauce
2 tbsps curry powder
1/2 tsp garlic salt
pinch of cayenne pepper
1 tbsp sugar
1/4 cup macadamia nuts, chopped
1/4 cup crisp bacon, crumbled

Peel, seed, and mash avocado with a fork.
Combine all ingredients and mix well.
Serve immediately or keep chilled and stir
again just before serving. Serves 6 to 8.

Sweets

Pineapple Upside-Down Cake

1/4 cup butter
1 cup brown sugar, firmly packed
3/4 cup pecans, chopped
1 can pineapple slices, drained, reserving 5 tbsps juice
3 eggs, separated
1 cup sugar
1 cup all-purpose flour
1 tsp baking powder
1/2 tsp salt
maraschino cherries

Melt butter and add brown sugar and pecans. Stir well then turn off heat. Arrange a single layer of pineapple slices in a greased baking pan and pour brown sugar and pecan mixture over the top. Combine flour, baking powder, and salt in a bowl; set aside. Beat egg yolks until thick and lemon colored. Gradually add the sugar, continuing to beat. Add the flour mixture to the yolk mixture and stir in the reserved pineapple juice. Beat the egg whites until stiff peaks form. Fold the whites into the cake batter. Pour or spoon the batter evenly over the pineapple slices. Bake at 350 degrees for 40 to 45 minutes. Cool the cake in the skillet for 30 minutes then invert it onto a serving plate. Place a maraschino cherry in the center of each pineapple ring. Serves 8.

Hawaiian Carrot Cake

2 cups flour
2 cups granulated sugar
1/2 tsp salt
1 tsp baking soda
1 1/2 tsps cinnamon
1/2 tsp nutmeg
3 eggs
1/2 cup vegetable oil
2 cups carrots, grated fine
1 1/2 tsps vanilla extract
8 oz. pineapple, crushed and drained well
1 cup flaked coconut
1/2 cup flaked coconut, lightly browned
1/2 cup pecans, finely chopped
1/2 cup macadamia nuts, coarsely chopped

Preheat oven to 350 degrees. Sift together first six ingredients. Add in this order: eggs, oil, carrots, and vanilla; mix well. Then fold in pineapple, one cup coconut, and pecans. Pour into a large rectangular, greased, 2-inch-deep pan. Bake for 60 minutes.

Frosting:
Beat cream cheese until smooth. Add butter and vanilla until completely blended. Gradually add powdered sugar. Remove cake from pan when cool and spread frosting on top and sides of cake. Sprinkle macadamia nuts and toasted coconut flakes on top as garnish. Serves 12-16.

Mango Cheesecake

2 pounds cream cheese, softened
1/2 cup sugar
1/4 pound unsalted butter, softened
4 large eggs
1 tsp vanilla
1 tbsp lime juice
3 tbsps flour
3 tbsps cornstarch
1 pound sour cream
1/2 cup mango puree (in food processor)
1 fresh mango, peeled and sliced

Preheat oven to 350 degrees. Butter a 9-inch spring form pan (w/approx. 3-inch sides). In a food processor, process cream cheese for 1 minute. Add sugar and softened butter until just mixed (about 15 seconds). Add eggs one at a time. Add vanilla, lime juice, flour, and cornstarch. Then add sour cream and mango puree, blending well. Pour the mixture into the spring form pan and bake for 60 minutes. Remove from oven and let rest for 1 hour. Refrigerate for 3 more hours. Before serving, remove sides of pan and garnish with mango slices. Serves 12.

Nut Nut Cookies

3/4 cup butter, softened
1 cup brown sugar, firmly packed
1 egg
3/4 cup macadamia nuts, finely chopped
1 tsp vanilla extract
1 3/4 cups all-purpose flour
1/2 tsp baking powder
1/4 tsp salt
1 cup grated coconut, toasted

Toast coconut:
Spread coconut in shallow pan. Bake at 350 degrees for about 15 minutes, stirring frequently, until lightly browned.

Cream the butter. Gradually add sugar and beat until light and fluffy. Beat egg, nuts, and vanilla into the butter mixture. Sift together flour, baking powder, and salt; add coconut. Combine butter and coconut mixture with dry ingredients, kneading with hands until the mixture is moistened and holds together. Chill in refrigerator for about 1 hour. Roll part of the dough out to 1/8-inch thickness and cut out with a cookie cutter. Bake on ungreased cookie sheet at 350 degrees for 12 to 14 minutes or until edges are golden brown. Makes about 50 to 60 cookies.

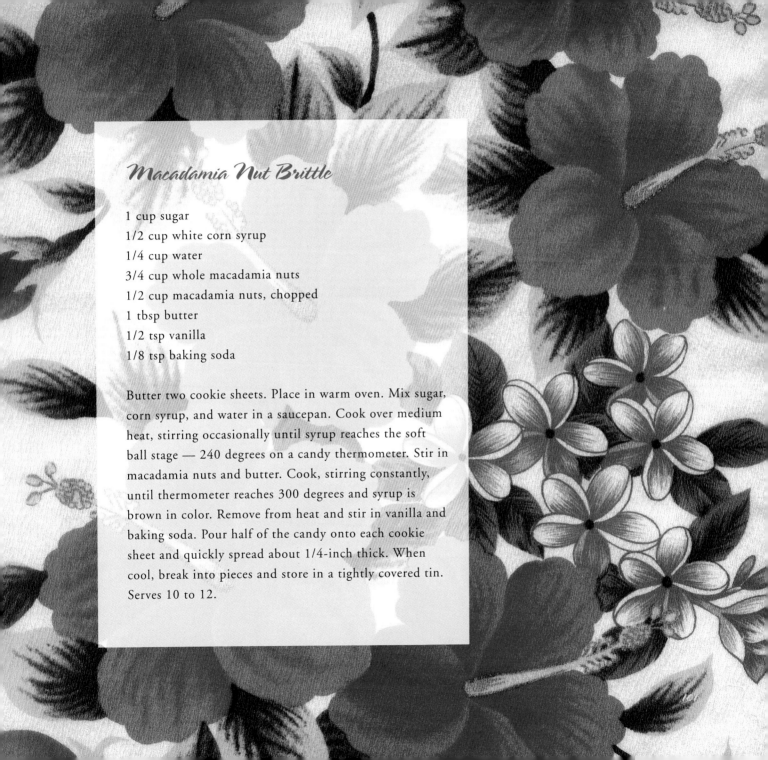

Macadamia Nut Brittle

1 cup sugar
1/2 cup white corn syrup
1/4 cup water
3/4 cup whole macadamia nuts
1/2 cup macadamia nuts, chopped
1 tbsp butter
1/2 tsp vanilla
1/8 tsp baking soda

Butter two cookie sheets. Place in warm oven. Mix sugar,
corn syrup, and water in a saucepan. Cook over medium
heat, stirring occasionally until syrup reaches the soft
ball stage — 240 degrees on a candy thermometer. Stir in
macadamia nuts and butter. Cook, stirring constantly,
until thermometer reaches 300 degrees and syrup is
brown in color. Remove from heat and stir in vanilla and
baking soda. Pour half of the candy onto each cookie
sheet and quickly spread about 1/4-inch thick. When
cool, break into pieces and store in a tightly covered tin.
Serves 10 to 12.

Almond Cookies

1 cup all-purpose flour
1 cup almonds, ground
1/4 tsp baking powder
pinch of salt
1/2 cup butter, softened
3/4 cup sugar
1 egg white
1/2 tsp almond extract

Sift together flour, baking powder, and salt. In a separate bowl, cream together butter and sugar. Add egg white and almond extract, mix well. Add the nuts in flour mixture and chill for an hour. Shape into 3/4-inch balls and place on a cookie sheet. Flatten slightly with the palm of your hand. Bake at 350 degrees for 12 to 15 minutes. Be sure they don't brown. Makes 4 dozen.

Macadamia Banana Bread

1 3/4 cups flour
1 tbsp baking powder
1/2 tsp salt
1 cup mashed bananas (2 large or 3 small ripe bananas)
1/2 cup butter
3/4 cup sugar
2 large eggs
1/2 cup macadamia nuts, finely chopped

Sift together flour, baking powder, and salt. Mash bananas
with a fork. Cream butter, add sugar, and beat until light
yellow. Add eggs one at a time and beat until smooth. Add
dry ingredients to creamed mixture. Then add banana and
mix well. Fold in nuts and pour into a buttered loaf pan.
Bake at 350 degrees for 45 to 50 minutes. Makes 1 loaf.

Tropical Fruit Squares

2 eggs
1/2 cup butter
3/4 cup sugar
3/4 cup flour
1 tsp baking powder
1/4 tsp salt
1/2 cup dates, chopped
1/2 cup nuts, chopped
1/2 cup coconut flakes
1/2 cup crushed pineapple (spread on
 paper towel to drain)
powdered or granulated sugar

Beat eggs until light and fluffy and gradually add sugar, continuing to beat. Sift together flour, baking powder, and salt. Add to the egg mixture and stir thoroughly. Fold in dates, nuts, coconut, and pineapple. Spread batter in well-greased pan and bake at 350 degrees for 30 to 35 minutes. While warm, cut into squares and roll in powdered sugar. Serves 15 to 20.

Chocolate Coconut Bars

3/4 cup brown sugar

1/2 cup granulated sugar

1/2 cup flour, sifted

1/4 tsp salt

2 eggs

2/3 cup flaked coconut

1/2 cup macadamia nuts, finely chopped

1/2 cup powdered sugar

1 1/2 squares (1 1/2 oz.) unsweetened
    chocolate, melted

Mix together flour, brown sugar, granulated
sugar, and salt. Add eggs, nuts, coconut, and
melted chocolate. Pour into greased 11 x 7 x
1 1/2-inch (2 quart) pan and bake at 350
degrees for about 25 minutes. Cut into strips
and roll in powdered sugar when cool.
Serves 15 to 20.

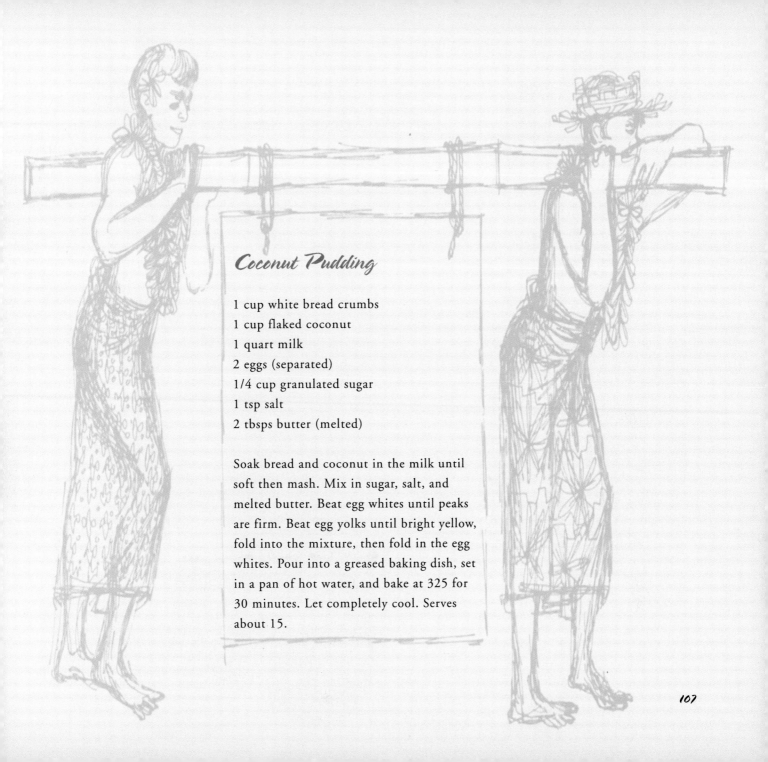

Coconut Pudding

1 cup white bread crumbs
1 cup flaked coconut
1 quart milk
2 eggs (separated)
1/4 cup granulated sugar
1 tsp salt
2 tbsps butter (melted)

Soak bread and coconut in the milk until
soft then mash. Mix in sugar, salt, and
melted butter. Beat egg whites until peaks
are firm. Beat egg yolks until bright yellow,
fold into the mixture, then fold in the egg
whites. Pour into a greased baking dish, set
in a pan of hot water, and bake at 325 for
30 minutes. Let completely cool. Serves
about 15.

Drinks

Rum Punch

3 oz. light rum
2 oz. orange juice
2 oz. guava juice
2 oz. pineapple juice
1/4 oz. grenadine
shaved ice

Mix all ingredients and pour over
ice in a chimney glass. Garnish
with a maraschino cherry, fresh
pineapple wedge, and mint leaf.
Serves 2.

Pali Punch

2 cups sugar
1 cup pineapple juice
1 cup guava juice
1/2 cup lime juice
1/2 cup brandy
1 quart champagne
chunks of ice or ice cubes
1 quart soda water

Dissolve sugar in pineapple and
guava juice. Mix lime juice with
brandy and champagne. Combine
both mixtures and pour over ice
in punch bowl. Add soda water.
Serves 10 to 12.

Lava Punch

1 fifth Southern Comfort
3/4 cup light rum
1 cup pineapple juice
1 cup grapefruit juice
3/4 cup lemon juice
2 bottles Brut champagne
1 oz. grenadine

Combine ingredients and pour over
chunks of ice. Serves about 25.

Planter's Punch

1 lime, juiced
2 oz. pineapple juice
2 oz. orange juice
2 oz. light rum
2 oz. 151-proof rum
1/2 oz. grenadine

Shake all ingredients well and pour
over ice in tall chimney glasses.
Garnish with a maraschino cherry and
orange slice. Serves 2.

Chi-Chi

1 1/2 oz. vodka
3 oz. pineapple juice
1 oz. crème de coconut
1 cup ice

Put all ingredients in blender and mix until
desired consistency. Serve in red wine glasses and garnish with pineapple slices and
cherries. Serves 2.

Guava Wine Cooler

1 quart rose wine
3/4 cup guava nectar
2 tbsps lemon juice
1 1/2 cups lemon-lime carbonated beverage

Chill first four ingredients and combine in
punch bowl; mix thoroughly. Garnish with
mint leaves and serve over ice. Makes 10 to 12
servings.

Frozen Fruit Daiquiris

1 1/2 oz. light rum
1/4 cup fruit (strawberries,
    bananas, etc.)
1 oz. fresh lime juice
1 tbsp powdered sugar
1 cup crushed ice

Put all ingredients in blender and
mix until desired consistency. Serve
in a champagne glass garnished with
a flower. Serves 1.

Cool Guava Colada

1 1/2 oz. dark rum
1 oz. crème de cocoa
3 oz. guava nectar
1 cup crushed ice

Mix in blender and pour into a red
wine glass. Garnish with a pineapple
wedge and flower. Serves 1.

Mai Tai

2 oz. dark rum
2 oz. light rum
1 oz. orange curacao
1/2 oz. orgeat syrup
1 lime, juiced
1/2 oz. simple syrup (50/50 sugar and
   water)

Shake all ingredients and pour over ice.
Garnish with wedges of pineapple and
mint sprigs. Serves 2.

Scorpion

2 limes, juiced
2 oz. fresh orange juice
2 oz. orgeat syrup
2 oz. brandy
2 oz. dark rum
2 oz. light rum
1 tbsp simple syrup (50/50 sugar and
    water)
shaved ice

Shake ingredients together and strain over
ice in white wine glasses. Garnish with
pineapple, maraschino cherries, and mint.
Serves 2.

Blue Hawaii

1 oz. light rum
1 oz. Blue Curacao
1 oz. crème de coconut
2 oz. pineapple juice
1 oz. simple syrup (50/50 sugar and water)

Put all ingredients in blender and mix until desired consistency. Pour into a highball glass and garnish with a pineapple slice and a maraschino cherry. Serves 1.

Sangria

1 bottle dry red wine
2 oz. Triple Sec
up to 1/2 cup sugar (to taste)
1 1/2 cups club soda
1 orange, juiced
1 lemon, thinly sliced
1 orange, thinly sliced

Mix all ingredients except sliced fruit. When sugar is dissolved, add sliced fruit and chill for 4 to 8 hours. Serve over ice in red wine glasses. Serves 8.

Tropical Itch

2 dashes of Angostura Bitters
1 oz. Orange Curacao
2 oz. vodka
2 oz. light rum
1/2 lime, juiced
8 oz. passion fruit juice
2 oz. 151-proof dark rum
shaved ice

Shake all ingredients with ice and pour
(with ice) into tall chimney glasses.
Garnish each with a maraschino cherry
and pineapple skewer and a tropical
flower. Serves 2.

Grasshopper

2 oz. crème de menthe
2 oz. crème de cocao
2 oz. heavy cream

Shake together with cracked ice.
Strain into cocktail glass and serve.
Serves 1.

Non-Alcoholic

Temptation Punch

6 cups passion fruit juice
12 cups guava juice
1 lemon, juiced
1 lime, juiced

Combine over large ice chunks in
a punch bowl. Garnish with mint.
Serves about 30.

Pineapple Sherbet Punch

5 cups orange juice
5 cups grapefruit juice
3 cups peach nectar
1 1/2 quarts ginger ale
1 1/2 quarts pineapple sherbet

Mix juices. Add ginger ale and sherbet
just before serving. Serves about 35.

Seaside Punch

6 cups pineapple juice
6 lemons, juiced
1 cup sugar
2 cups cranberry juice
8 cups ginger ale
1 pint pineapple sherbet

Mix first four ingredients. Add ginger ale and sherbet just before serving. Garnish with pineapple chunks and maraschino cherries. Serves 20 to 25.

Shirley Temple Punch

1 liter lemon-lime carbonated beverage
3 tbsps grenadine
20 maraschino cherries

Mix all ingredients and pour into a pitcher. Stir before serving over ice in tall glasses. Serves 8 to 10.

Hawaiian Punch

6 cups guava juice
6 cups papaya juice
6 cups pineapple juice
1 lemon, juiced
1/3 cup sugar

Combine over large ice chunks in a punch bowl. Serves about 30.

Luau Iced Tea

4 to 5 sprigs of fresh mint
1 gallon prepared tea
3 cups sugar
3 cups water
6 lemons, juiced

Add mint leaves to tea and allow
to stand 30 minutes then remove.
Combine sugar, water, and lemon
juice and add to tea. Chill thoroughly. Serve over ice cubes in
tall glasses. Garnish with mint.
Serves 25.

Cranberry Cooler

2 tbsps crushed pineapple
2 tbsps lemon juice
1 1/2 cups cranberry juice cocktail
1 1/2 cups ginger ale

Combine first three ingredients into
chimney glasses with ice then fill with
ginger ale. Serves 2 to 3.

Pineapple Slide

32 oz. orange juice
32 oz. lemonade
6 pints pineapple sherbet
1 quart vanilla ice cream

Break apart sherbet and ice cream in a
punch bowl, leaving large pieces. Add fruit
juices and mix to partially melt sherbet
and ice cream. Garnish with orange and
pineapple rings. Serves 25 to 30.

125

Index